W9-CFV-497

2

Scott Foresman

Accelerating English Language Learning

Authors
Anna Uhl Chamot
Jim Cummins
Carolyn Kessler
J. Michael O'Malley
Lily Wong Fillmore

Consultant
George González

Longman

ACKNOWLEDGMENTS

Illustrations Unless otherwise acknowledged, all illustrations are the property of Scott, Foresman and Company. Page abbreviations are as follows: (T) top, (B) bottom, (L) left, (R) right, (C) center.

Elizabeth Allen 26–27, 45(B), 47, 48–51; Shannon Brickey 52; Nan Brooks 88–99; Michael Carroll 32–35, 54(L), 55(TR), 56(B), 57, 77(B), 102(B), 103(TR), 116(T), 118(L), 118(R), 123(T), 139(B), 142(R), 149, 156, 192–193, 216–217(B), 223(B), 224(B), 225(B), 229(B); Jessica Clerk 58, 59(T), 76, 86–87, 100, 144, 152; Carolyn Croll 183, 190; Bob Dorsey 82(T), 83(T), 106; Kathi Ember 6–7, 25(B), 104–105, 228; Mike Hagel 41(B), 42(B), 45(L), 46(B), 53(B); Herman Adler Design Group 36, 37, 39(B), 50(T), 138, 150, 151, 219, 222, 227; Lily Hong 188–189; Jeff Kaufman 147; Linda Kelen 62–63; Fran Lee 24, 112–113, 115(B), 186-187, 191(B); Anne Lunsford 38, 79(T), 101(C), 176; Donna Nelson 140-141, 143, 153(B); Corasue Nicholas 4(T), 5(T), 11; Michele Noiset 119; Cheryl Roberts 194(T), 195(T), 221; Walter Stuart 10, 30–31, 82(B), 83(B), 120–121, 198, 199; Kat Thacker 155(C), 161(T); U.S. Mapping Specialists 8–9, 196–197; Marsha Winborn 114, 214.

Literature 12-23: MY PERFECT NEIGHBORHOOD by Leah Komaiko, Illustrations by Barbara Westman. Copyright © 1990 by Leah Komaiko, illustrations copyright © by Barbara Westman. Reprinted by permission of Harper Collins Publishers. 64-75: From WHEN I'M HUNGRY by Jane R. Howard, illustrated by Teri Sloat. Copyright © 1992 by Jane R. Howard, text. Copyright © 1992 by Teri Sloat, illustrations. Reprinted by permission of Dutton Children's Books, a division of Penguin Books USA Inc. 126-137: BREAD IS FOR EATING by David and Phillis Gershator. Copyright © 1995 Henry Holt and Company, Inc. Reprinted by permission. 164-175: NINE O'CLOCK LULLABY by Marilyn Singer, Illustrations by Frane Lessac. Copyright © 1991 Marilyn Singer, Illustrations copyright © 1991 Frane Lessac. Reprinted by permission of Harper Collins Publishers. 202-213: "Brave Dog" from HENRY AND MUDGE AND THE FOREVER SEA by Cynthia Rylant. Copyright © 1989 Bradbury Press, an affiliate of Macmillan Inc. Reprinted by permission.

Poems and Songs 24: "Merry-Go-Round" from THE WHEELS OF THE BUS GO ROUND AND ROUND by Nancy Larrick. Text Copyright © 1972 by Nancy Larrick. Published by Childrens Press. Reprinted by permission of Grolier Publishing Co. 38: "Polar Bear" by Nita Jonas from THE WILD WOOLLY BOOK. Copyright © 1961 Random House. Reprinted by permission. 100: "Al Tambor/The Drum Song" from DE COLORES AND OTHER LATIN AMERICAN FOLK SONGS... by Jose Luis Orozco. Copyright © 1994 by Jose Luis Orozco. Reprinted by permission of Dutton Children's Books, a division of Penguin Books USA Inc. 114: "Pulling and pushing..." from MOTHER GOOSE ON THE RIO GRANDE by Frances Alexander.

Copyright © 1988 by Passport Books, a division of NTC Publishing Corp. Reprinted by permission. 147: "Get 'Em Here" from MUNCHING: POEMS ABOUT EATING by Lee Bennett Hopkins. Copyright © 1970 by Lee Bennett Hopkins. Reprinted by permission of Curtis Brown Ltd. 152: "Growing Songs" from FOUR CORNERS OF THE SKY by Theodore Clymer. Text copyright © 1975 by Theodore Clymer. Reprinted by permission of Little, Brown and Company.

161: "Old Man Moon" from IN THE WOODS, IN THE MEADOW, IN THE SKY by Aileen Fisher. Text copyright © 1965 by Aileen Fisher. Reprinted by permission of the author. 176: "Out in the Dark and Daylight" from OUT IN THE DARK AND DAYLIGHT by Aileen Fisher. Text copyright © 1980 by Aileen Fisher. Reprinted by permission of the author. 214: "Sitting In The Sand" from DOGS & DRAGONS, TREES & DREAMS by Karla Kuskin. Copyright © 1980 by Karla Kuskin. Reprinted by permission of Harper Collins Publishers. 228: "Raindrops" from SING AND BE HAPPY by Clara Belle Baker. Copyright renewed 1949 by Clara Belle Baker. Reprinted by permission of the publisher, Abingdon Press.

Photography Unless otherwise acknowledged, all photographs are the property of Scott, Foresman and Company. Page abbreviations are as follows: (T) top, (C) center, (B) bottom, (R) right.

v PhotoEdit; 2(t) David Young-Wolff/PhotoEdit; 3(tl) Tony Freeman/PhotoEdit; 3(br) David Young-Wolff/PhotoEdit; 5 Tony Freeman/PhotoEdit; 28(tl, tr, bl, br), 29(tl, tr, cl, br) Superstock, Inc.; (bl) Rhoda Sidney/PhotoEdit; 40(t) Terry Vine/Tony Stone Images; 41(b), 43(tr, b), 44(tl, tr ,bl) Superstock, Inc.; (br) Ted Wood/Black Star; 46(t) Richard Hutchings/PhotoEdit; (bl) Erica Lansner/Black Star; 48(b) Superstock, Inc.; 54 Zig Leszczynski/Animals Animals; 55(r) J.A.L. Cooke/Oxford Scientific Films/Animals Animals; (t) Betty K. Bruce/Animals Animals; 56 Richard Kolar/Animals Animals; 59 E.R. Degginger/Animals Animals; 61(b) Superstock, Inc.; (t) Bates Littlehales/Animals Animals; 80(cr) Mary Kate Denny/PhotoEdit; (t) Myrleen Ferguson/PhotoEdit; 81(cr) Myrleen Ferguson Cate/PhotoEdit; 84(t) Superstock, Inc.; (bl) Mary Kate Denny/PhotoEdit; 102 Superstock, Inc.; 103(t) Superstock, Inc.; 110(t) Skjold/PhotoEdit; (c) Elizabeth Zuckerman/PhotoEdit; (bl) Tony Freeman/PhotoEdit; 116(b) Grant Heilman Photography; 117(bl) Holt Confer/Grant Heilman Photography; 118(c) Superstock, Inc.; (bl) Superstock, Inc.; (br) Grant Heilman/Grant Heilman Photography; 141(b) Michael Newman/PhotoEdit; (t) Tony Freeman/PhotoEdit; 142(m) Agricultural Research Service, USDA; (b) Jose Carrillo/PhotoEdit; (t) Cy Furlan; 145(b) Rhoda Sidney/PhotoEdit; (t) Robert Frerck; 146(tr) Michelle Bridwell/PhotoEdit; (tr) Michael Newman/PhotoEdit; 157(t, b) Myrleen Ferguson/PhotoEdit; 158(b) Superstock, Inc.; (t) NASA; 162 Corbis-Bettmann Archive; 163 Robert Frerck/Odyssey Productions/Chicago; 178(l) Photo Researchers; 179(tl) Ann Purcell '89/Photo Researchers; 180 Brown Brothers; 182 Michael Felice Corne, "Landing of the Pilgrims," 1806/Pilgrim Society; 184(b) Tony Freeman/PhotoEdit; (t) Porterfield/Chickering/Photo Researchers; 185 Wide World; 192(b) Dick Luria/FPG International Corp.; 193(b) David Young-Wolff/PhotoEdit; (tr) Tony Freeman/PhotoEdit; 195 Photri, Inc.; 198 Doug Wilson/Westlight; Art Wolfe/Tony Stone Images; 199 Kennon Cooke/Valan Photos; 200(br) John Eastcott/VVA Monatiuk/Valan Photos; (bl) Tony Stone Images; (t) Charles McNulty/Tony Stone Images; 216(t) Tom McCarthy/Unicorn Stock Photos; (b) Robert Brenner/PhotoEdit; 217(t) Robert Brenner/PhotoEdit; (b); Cindy Charles/PhotoEdit; 218(c) Wouterloot-Gregoire/Valan Photos; (l) Don McPhee/Valan Photos; (l) Superstock, Inc.; 224 Doug Wilson/Westlight; 225 Kennon Cooke/Valan Photos.

CONSULTANTS

Sandra H. Bible
Elementary ESL Teacher
Shawnee Mission School District
Shawnee Mission, Kansas

Anaida Colón-Muñiz, Ed.D.
Director of English Language
Development
and Bilingual Education
Santa Ana Unified School District
Santa Ana, California

Debbie Corkey-Corber
Educational Consultant
Williamsburg, Virginia

Barbara Crandall
Carol Baranyi
Ilean Zamlut
ESOL Teachers
Lake Park Elementary School
Palm Beach County, Florida

Lily Pham Dam
Instructional Specialist
Dallas Independent School District
Dallas, Texas

María Delgado
Milwaukee Public Schools
Milwaukee, Wisconsin

Dr. M. Viramontes de Marín
Chair, Department of Education and
Liberal Studies at the National
Hispanic University
San Jose, California

Virginia Hansen
ESOL Resource Teacher
Palm Beach County, Florida

Tim Hart
Supervisor of English as a Second
Language
Wake County
Releigh, North Carolina

Lilian I. Jezik
Bilingual Resource Teacher
Corona-Norco Unified School District
Norco, California

Helen L. Lin
Chairman, Education Program
Multicultural Arts Council of
Orange County, California
Formerly ESL Lab Director,
Kansas City, Kansas Schools

Justine McDonough
Trish Lirio
Sheree Di Donato
Jupiter Elementary School
West Palm Beach, Florida

Teresa Montaña
United Teachers Los Angeles
Los Angeles, California

Loriana M. Novoa, Ed.D.
Research and Evaluation Consultants
Miami, Florida

Beatrice Palls
ESOL and Foreign Language
Supervisor
Pasco County, Florida

Rosa María Peña
Austin Independent School District
Austin, Texas

Alice Quarles
Assistant Principal
Fairlawn Elementary School
Dade County, Florida

Thuy Pham-Remmele
ESL/Bilingual K–12 Specialist
Madison Metropolitan School District
Madison, Wisconsin

Jacqueline J. Servi Margis
ESL and Foreign Language
Curriculum Specialist
Milwaukee Public Schools
Milwaukee, Wisconsin

Carmen Sorondo
Supervisor, ESOL, K–12
Hillsborough County, Florida

Susan C. VanLeuven
Poudre R-1 School District
Fort Collins, Colorado

Rosaura Villaseñor
(Educator)
Norwalk, California

Cheryl Wilkinson
J. O. Davis Elementary School
Irving Independent School District
Irving, Texas

Phyllis I. Ziegler
ESL/Bilingual Consultant
New York, New York

TABLE OF CONTENTS

People and Places

Tell what you know.

What is a **group?**

What kinds of groups are these?

Talk About It

Tell about a group you are part of.

Name other groups you know.

What can these groups do?

Family **members** share things.

Class members make things together.

Team members play a game together.

Neighbors help each other.

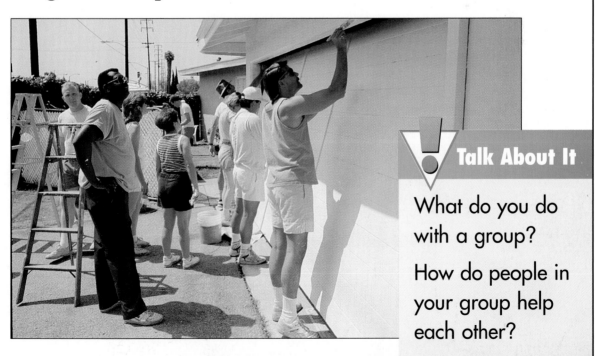

Talk About It

What do you do with a group?

How do people in your group help each other?

What is a community?

Groups of people live and work in a **community.**

A community has homes and other buildings.

What places do you see in this community?

What places are in your community?

The United States of America

This **country** is the United States of America.

The United States has 50 **states**. A state is an area with many communities.

The United States

CANA[DA]

WASHINGTON

MONTANA

NORTH DAKOTA

OREGON

IDAHO

SOUTH DAKOTA

WYOMING

NEBRASKA

NEVADA

UTAH

COLORADO

KANSAS

CALIFORNIA

OKLAHOMA

ARIZONA

NEW MEXICO

TEXAS

PACIFIC OCEAN

ARCTIC OCEAN

HAWAII

RUSSIA

ALASKA

CANADA

MEXICO

Bering Sea

PACIFIC OCEAN

GULF OF ALASKA

Point to Indiana on the map.
Which states are next to Indiana?

Point to Colorado on the map.
Which states are next to Colorado?

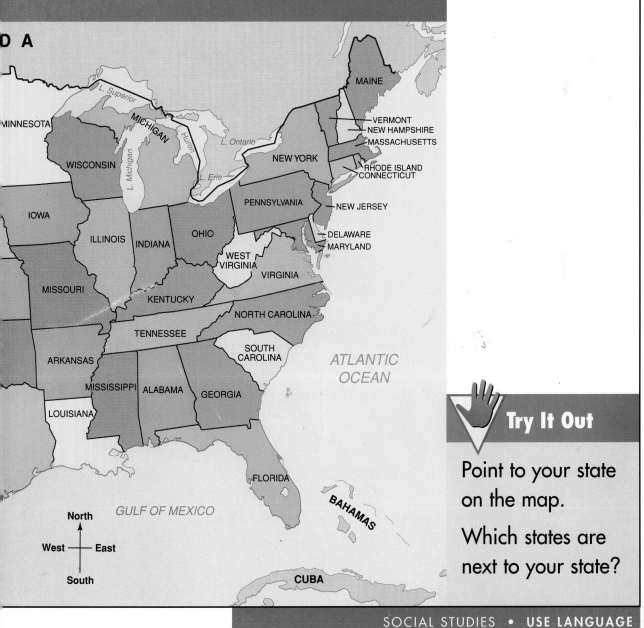

Try It Out

Point to your state on the map.

Which states are next to your state?

Where do animals live?

What animals live in trees?

What animals live in water?

Some animals live in a forest.

blue jays ▶

▲ deer

squirrels ▶

▲ foxes

Some animals live in a pond.

frogs ▲

▼ ducks

▼ turtles

fish ▼

? Think About It

Why is a pond a good place for a frog to live?

Tell about another animal and where it lives.

My Perfect Neighborhood

written by
Leah Komaiko

illustrated by
Barbara Westman

I went out for a walk today.
My neighborhood she looked okay.

The dogs waved when
the cats marched by.

The builders built a brick-cream pie

And clothes hung in the trees to dry.
My neighborhood's the place to try.

I went out for a walk today.

My neighborhood she looked okay.

The grown-ups lined up for recess.

The poodles found a wedding dress

And birds played bongos, more or less.
This neighborhood's the best address.

I went out for my walk today.
My neighborhood she looked okay.
A horse was out on roller skates.

My grandmother was lifting weights
And dishwashers were juggling plates.
I told you, this place really rates.

I went out for my walk today
And saw the sights that came my way:
The dentist shaving someone's head,

The baker baking sweet-tooth bread,
And bed salesmen, asleep in bed.
This place is special, like I said.

I went out for my walk today
And saw . . . *myself* . . . I looked okay.

My legs were each a half arm high.
My elbow almost touched my thigh
And half my nose was in my eye.
Oh, what a gorgeous girl am I!

I love my walks, for then I see
That things are just as they should be.

Merry - Go - Round

The more we get together,
Together, together,
The more we get together
The happier we'll be.

For your friends are my friends,
And my friends are your friends,
The more we get together
The happier we'll be.

Tell what you learned.

1. What groups are you part of?

2. Write a list of places in a community. Put a check next to each place you see in your community.

In My Community
library
park
✓school

3. Draw a picture. Show something the girl in the story saw in her neighborhood.

Animals and Their Habitats

Tell what you know.

What animals are these?

What are they doing?

geese ▲

cats ▲

▼ sheep

ducks ▼

cows ▶

Talk About It

Tell about other animals you know.

What do they do?

What animals are there?

Word Bank

ants

bear

butterfly

dog

eagle

goldfish

lion

parrot

shark

Name these animals.

Fish live in the water.

Birds have feathers.

Insects have six legs.

Mammals have hair or fur.

❓ Think About It

Which animals can be pets?

Would a lion make a good pet? Why? Why not?

What does an animal get from its habitat?

A **habitat** is a place where plants and animals live.

An animal gets food and water from its habitat.

An animal gets air from its habitat.

butterfly

cats

An animal raises its family in its habitat.

What animals do you see in this habitat?

rabbits ▼

quail

Talk About It

What do these birds get from their habitat?

A Pet and Its Habitat

A habitat for a pet should have food, water, and air.

Choose a pet you would like to have.

hamster

fish

parakeet

Which habitat would be good for your pet?

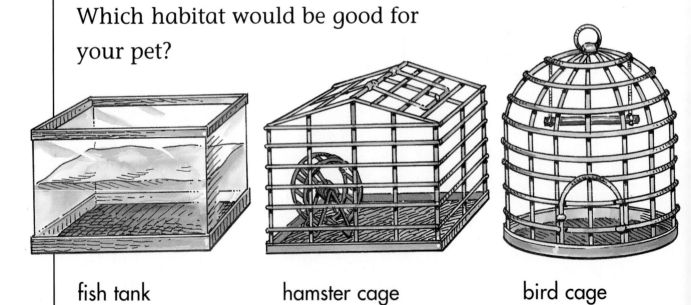

fish tank

hamster cage

bird cage

Which food would be good for
your pet?

fruits and vegetables   fish food   bird seed

Does each habitat have the food,
water, and air the pet needs?

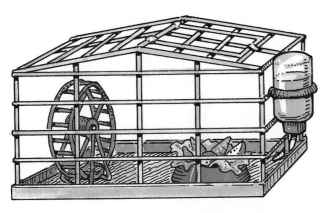

Write About It

Draw the pet you
chose and its
habitat. Write
how the pet will
get what it needs
from its habitat.

How many in all?

How many monkeys are in the trees?

How many birds are in the trees?

Count all the animals in the trees.
How many are there?

bird ▼

▼ snake

How many monkeys are there in all?

How many lizards are there in all?

Are there more monkeys or more lizards?

Write a number sentence about animals.

monkey

lizard

Talk About It

How many animals do you see in all?

Which animals have you seen or read about?

An Animal Riddle

by Faisal Al Shatti, age 10

I am as sneaky as a fox.
I am as long as the neck of a giraffe.
I am as lazy as a snail.
I am as tricky as a wolf.
I am as slow as a turtle.
I am as slimy as a frog.
I am as quiet as an ant.
I live in somewhere green.
. . . I am a "SNAKE."

An Animal Riddle

by Abdulla Al Kulaib, age 10

I am as fat as an elephant.

I am as gray as a mouse.

I am as lazy as a bear in winter.

I am as large as a log.

I am as smooth as a snake.

My mouth is as wide as a football.

My ears are as small as an egg.

My legs are as small as a shoe.

My head is as tall as a bottle.

My eyes are as round as a knot.

I am a hippopotamus.

Polar Bear

by Nita Jonas

In the cold, cold North
    where there's snow in the air
Lives the white, fuzzy,
    furry polar bear.
He's a very good swimmer
    and he thinks it's nice
To take a nap
    on a block of ice!

Try It Out

Pretend you are a polar bear. See if your classmates can guess what you are doing.

Tell what you learned.

1. Make a chart. Write the name of an animal for each group.

Animal Group	Animal Name
insects	ant
fish	
mammals	
birds	

2. Name an animal. Tell what it gets from its habitat.

3. Make up your own riddle about an animal. Draw and describe the animal in your riddle.

CHAPTER 3

How People Work

Tell what you know.

Who are these people?

What do they do to help other people?

Talk About It

Which of these workers have you seen in your community?

What other workers do you see in your community?

How do these workers help us?

Name these **workers**.
What do they do?

Some workers collect garbage.
Some workers deliver mail.

garbage collector ▲

mail carrier ▶

Some workers help us find books in the library.
Some workers help us when we are hurt.
Some workers keep us safe.

▲ **lifeguard**

▲ **librarian**

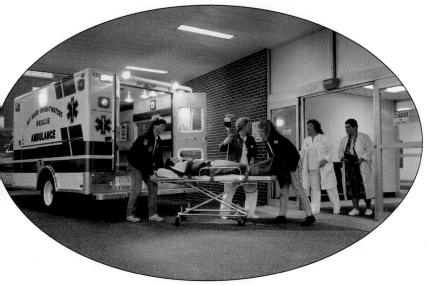

▲ **paramedic**

Talk About It

Name some other jobs community workers do.

What community job would you like to do?

Where do other workers work?

bank

factory

farm

office

▲ factory workers   ▲ office worker

▲ bank teller   ▲ farmer

Some people do not work in just one place. This worker goes from place to place to fix TVs.

▲ TV repair person

What other workers go from place to place?

What do you want to be when you grow up?

Talk About It

Where do people in your family work?

What are needs and wants?

Needs are the things you cannot live without. People need food, water, clothing, and a place to live.

Wants are things you would like to have. You might want a bike or a video game.

How do people get things they need and want?

People earn money for the work they do.

They use the money to buy things they need and want.

They can save some money too.

Think About It

What things would you like to have?

How could you save money to get them?

Do animals have the same needs as people?

Word Bank

armadillo

cardinal

fish

robins

squirrel

People need food, water, and a place to live.

They need clothing too.

People have thin, smooth skin.

Animals need food, water, and a place to live. Animals do not need clothing because they have thick coverings. Fur or hair, feathers, scales, or shells cover animals.

Animal	Covering
cat	fur or hair
duck	
turtle	
goldfish	

Write About It

Make a chart.
Write the animal's covering:
feathers, fur or hair, scales, shell.

What I Want to Do

by Cristina Ruiz, age 8
I want to learn English because I want to be a teacher. I like to help children. I like to help my grandmother. I like to help my baby brother.

My Family Works

by Xing Chen Mai, age 7
My name is Xing Chen Mai. I am seven years old. I came to America with my Mom in a big airplane. I came from China.

My dad works very hard. He is studying for his doctor's degree in engineering at Cleveland State University. My mom works, too. She works in a Chinese restaurant. She goes to school to learn English.

When I grow up, I want to be a police officer. I want to help people and protect the city.

I love America!

A Gardener's Song

Lyrics by Frank Muschal
Music Traditional

This is the way
Our garden will grow.
We'll plant, we'll water,
We'll weed, we'll hoe.
And we will see
Our flowers grow,
As our reward for working.

? Think About It

Sing the song again.
Think of other places to sing about.

Tell what you learned.

CHAPTER 3

1. Make a list of community workers. Put a check next to the ones you have seen.

> **Workers**
> ✓ police officer
> garbage collector
> street cleaner

2. Work with a partner. Take turns naming an animal and saying if it is covered with fur or hair, feathers, scales, or a shell.

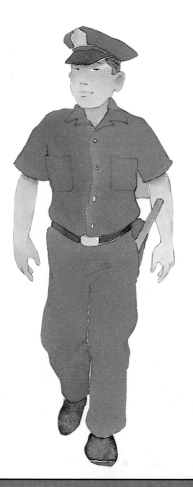

3. Draw a picture. Show one of the workers that Xing Chen Mai or Cristina Ruiz wrote about.

What Animals Do

Tell what you know.

Can you name these animals?

What kinds of work are they doing?

◀ **butterfly**

squirrel ▶

spider ▼

▼ ants

bird ▲

Talk About It

Which animals are getting food?

Which animals are making a home?

How do some animals work?

Animals work in different ways. They work to meet their **needs.**

Bees make honeycombs. Then they make honey. They store the honey in their honeycombs.

Beavers cut down small trees. They use some of the wood to build a dam. They use some of the wood to build a home.

▲ honeycomb, honey

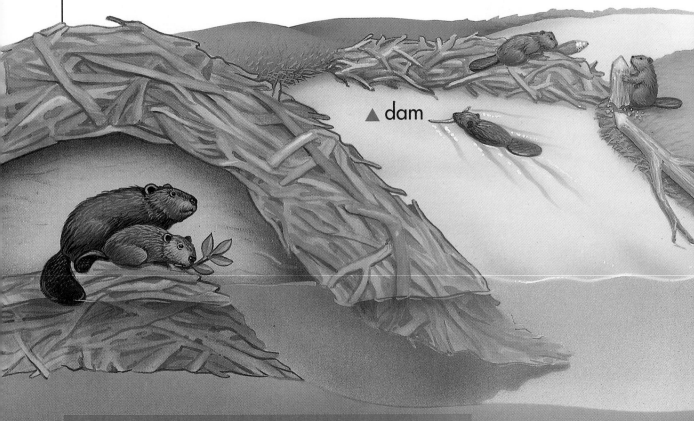

▲ dam

Woodchucks dig tunnels under the ground. They use their front feet to dig the dirt. They use their back feet to push the dirt out. They live inside the tunnels they build.

tunnel

Try It Out

Work with a group. Take turns acting out an animal working. Have others in your group guess the animal.

What do animals do to protect themselves?

Animals need to **protect** themselves from other animals.

A skunk can protect itself from another animal. It sprays the animal with a bad smell.

A turtle can protect itself from another animal. It hides inside its shell.

A rabbit can protect itself from another animal. It runs very fast.

A chameleon can protect itself from another animal. It changes its color.

Can you see the chameleon on the tree?

Word Bank

claws

teeth

fly

jump

Talk About It

What animal do you like?

How does it protect itself from other animals?

Color can make things hard to see.

Follow these steps.

1. Use two small pieces of white paper. Draw and cut out two rabbits.

2. Use two small pieces of brown paper. Draw and cut out two rabbits.

3. Put a white rabbit and a brown rabbit on a large piece of brown paper.

4. Put a white rabbit and a brown rabbit on a large piece of white paper.

5. Keep a record. What did you see?

My Record

1. It was harder to see the white rabbit ____.

2. It was harder to see the brown rabbit ____.

Think About It

Name other animals whose colors make them hard to see.

How many are there now?

There were seven birds in the grass. Three flew away. How many are in the grass now?

There were nine fish in the tank. Six fish were sold. How many are in the tank now?

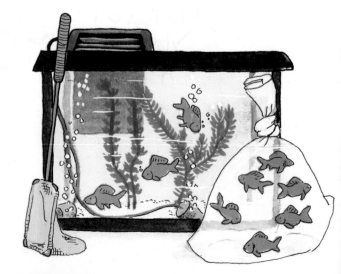

There were five bees on a leaf. One flew away. How many are on the leaf now?

There were three armadillos by the road. One ran away. How many are by the road now?

Write About It

Make up a problem about animals. End your problem with this question. How many are there now?

When I'm Hungry

written by Jane R. Howard

illustrated by Teri Sloat

When I'm hungry and eat my breakfast,
sometimes I wish I could

eat my fruit right off the tree

or sip juicy nectar from a flower

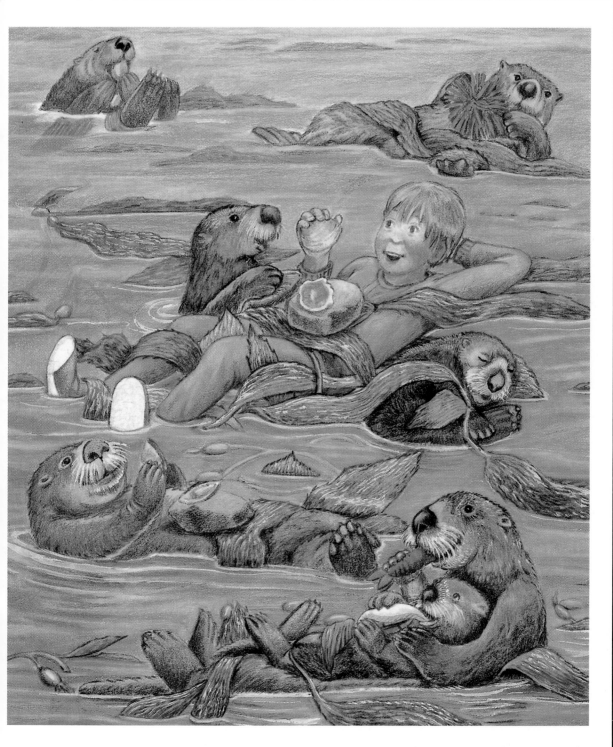

or float on my back with my food on my stomach

or maybe store it in my cheeks

or eat it underwater.

When I'm hungry for my morning snack, I wonder how it would feel to lap with my tongue or use it to catch my food.

When I'm hungry, I sometimes think
I'd like to eat my lunch in the mud

or with my mouth wide open.

When I'm hungry in the afternoon, I'm glad I don't have to dive for my food or dig for wiggly worms or get my honey from a tree.

And I'm glad I don't have to eat
eucalyptus leaves or bamboo shoots.

When I'm hungry at dinnertime, I'm happy to eat from my very own plate and drink from my very own glass, right in the middle of my very own family.

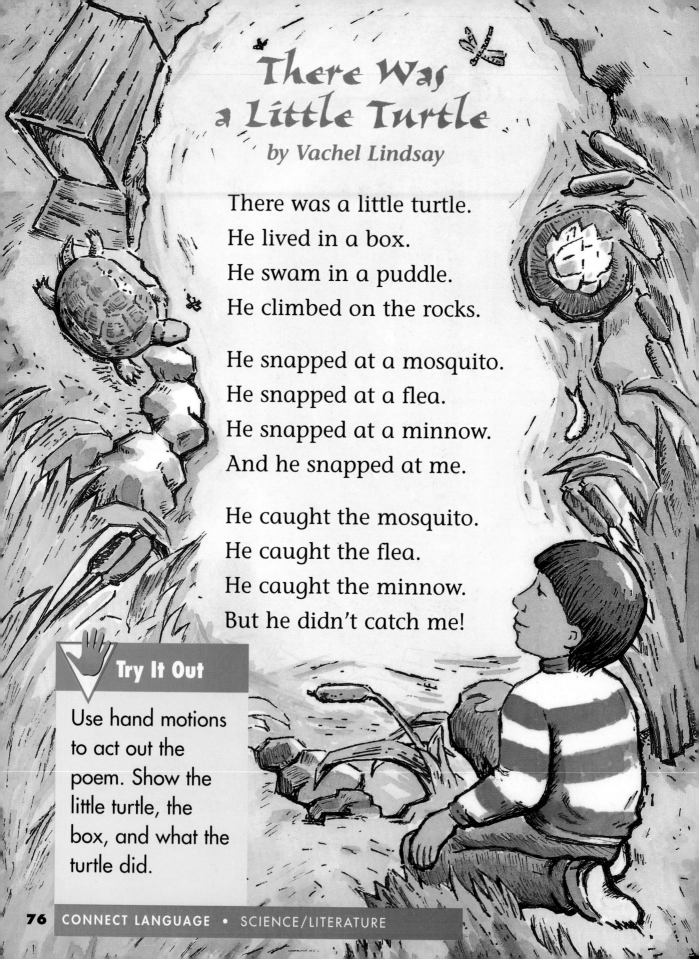

There Was a Little Turtle

by Vachel Lindsay

There was a little turtle.
He lived in a box.
He swam in a puddle.
He climbed on the rocks.

He snapped at a mosquito.
He snapped at a flea.
He snapped at a minnow.
And he snapped at me.

He caught the mosquito.
He caught the flea.
He caught the minnow.
But he didn't catch me!

Try It Out

Use hand motions to act out the poem. Show the little turtle, the box, and what the turtle did.

Tell what you learned.

1. Make a chart. Work together.
Write the name of an animal.
Write what it does.

Animal	Work
bird	builds nests

2. How do animals protect
themselves?

3. Work together. Draw a picture
to show where an animal
in the story gets its food.
Tell other classmates about
your picture.

How We Have Fun

Tell what you know.

What toys have you played with?

▼ drum

◀ bubbles

ball ▼

doll ◀

teddy bear ◀

blocks ◀

toy train ▲

▼ toy car

Playing Alone

You can play alone.
It can be fun to play alone.

Playing with Friends

To play some games you need one friend.

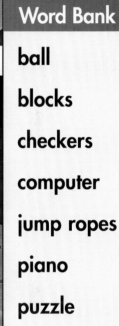

To play other games you need more than one friend.

Word Bank

ball

blocks

checkers

computer

jump ropes

piano

puzzle

Talk About It

What do you like to do alone?

What do you like to do with friends?

Having fun can help you stay healthy.

Do you get **exercise** while you play?

You need exercise to make you **strong**. Exercise can be fun.

swimming

hopping ▶

running ▶

Running, hopping, and swimming are good for your heart and lungs.

lungs —

heart —

standing ▶
up straight

stretching ▶

Stretching and standing up straight as you walk are good for your **muscles**.

Talk About It

How do you get exercise?

Tell how your exercise is good for you.

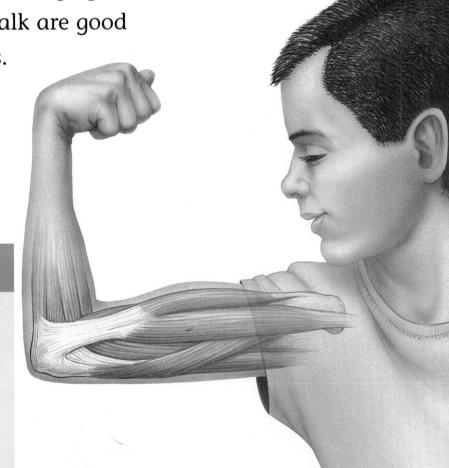

You use your body when you play.

Word Bank

arms

ears

eyes

feet

hands

legs

Which parts of the body are these children using?

soccer ▲

tennis ▲

swimming ▲

Use your eyes and hands.

Play "Follow the Leader" with a friend.

1. Be the Leader. Do not speak.
Show these hand motions.
  clap, clap, snap, snap,
  wave, wave, knock, knock

2. Your friend should do
what you do.

3. Take turns being
the Leader. Make up
motions of your own.

Think About It

Name something
you do at home
or at school.

What parts of
your body do
you use?

How many?

Hilda brought 2 toy cars to the birthday party. Marc brought 1 toy car. How many toy cars were there in all?

Pablo and Rosa played catch. Then Su came to play with them. How many children played catch in all?

Leah had 9 red checkers. She gave
3 red checkers to her sister.
How many were left?

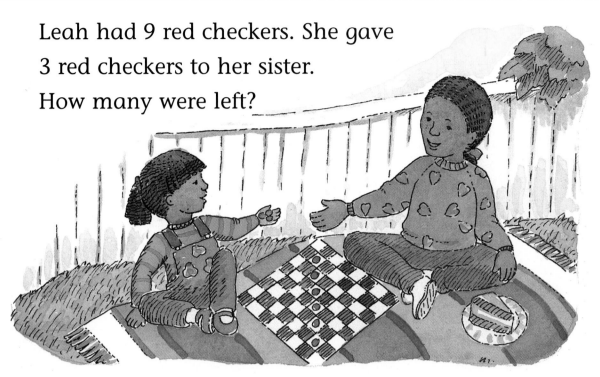

There were 8 balloons at the party.
Lee took 2 balloons home.
How many were left?

Write About It

Make up a problem. End your problem with this question. How many were left?

When We All Go Out and Play

adapted from Mother Goose

What will we do when we all go out,
All go out, all go out?

What will we do when we all go out,
When we all go out to play?

You can push the merry-go-round,
The merry-go-round, the merry-go-round.

Then I will push the merry-go-round,
When we all go out to play.

I will pull and you can ride,
You can ride, you can ride.

Then you will pull and I can ride,
When we all go out to play.

I will push and you can swing,
You can swing, you can swing.

You will push and I can swing,
When we all go out to play.

We'll climb up and then slide down,
Then slide down, then slide down.

We'll climb up and then slide down,
When we all go out to play.

We will have a lot of fun,
A lot of fun, a lot of fun.

We will have a lot of fun,
When we all go out to play.

PLAY THE DRUM

Translated by José-Luis Orozco

Play the drum, play the drum,
Play the drum from Panama,
Come on let's play the drum
Tum, tum, tum,
La, la, la, la, la.

María, Oh! María
María, my dear friend,
It's time to sing and dance
With the drum tum, tum,
La, la, la.

Try It Out

Sing the song
again and again.
Each time, name
someone in your
class.

Tell What You Learned.

1. Name something you like to do alone. Name something you like to do with a friend.

2. Draw a picture of yourself getting exercise. Label the parts of your body you are using.

3. Work in groups. Make a book of things you like to do on the playground. Tell other groups about your book.

How Things Move

Tell what you know.

Can you name things that move?

Where do you see them?

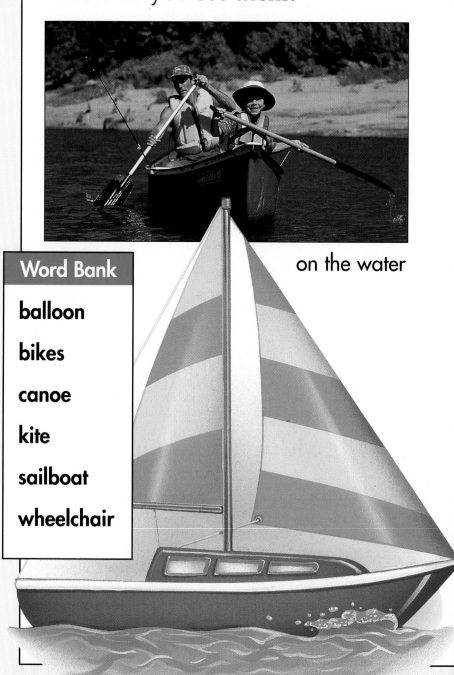

on the water

Word Bank

balloon

bikes

canoe

kite

sailboat

wheelchair

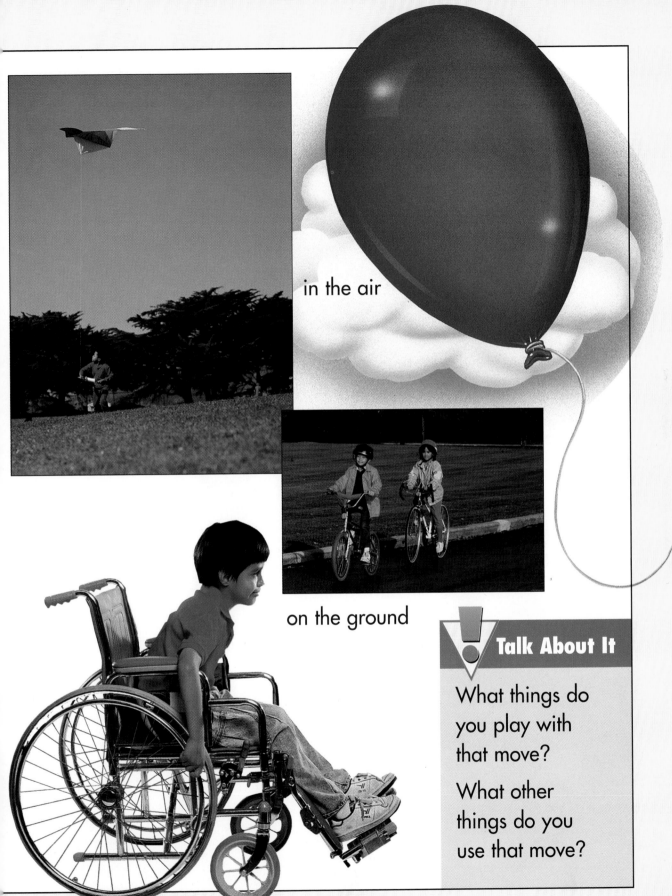

in the air

on the ground

Talk About It

What things do
you play with
that move?

What other
things do you
use that move?

What can you push and pull?

What can you push?

What can you pull?

Word Bank

merry-go-round

stroller

toy

toy truck

wagon

Try It Out

Look around your classroom.
What things can you push or pull?

What makes things move?

Force makes things move. You use force when you push open a door. You use force when you pull up your sock.

What have you moved today?
How did you move it?

Use force to move things.

Find out about it.

1. Put 2 trucks at the starting line.

2. Use a gentle push to make the first truck go.

3. Use a hard push to make the second truck go.

My Record

When I gave the truck a gentle push _____.

When I gave the truck a hard push _____.

4. Use tape. Mark the place where each truck stopped.

! Talk About It

Which truck went farther? Why?

What do magnets do?

Things You Need

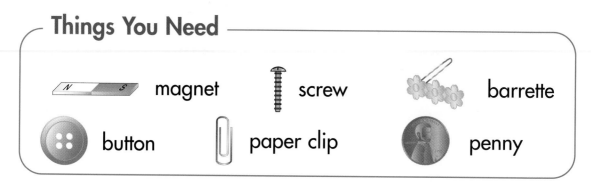

magnet   screw   barrette

button   paper clip   penny

Find out about it.

1. Hold the magnet over the button. What happens?

2. Hold the magnet over the penny. What happens?

3. Hold the magnet over the paper clip. What happens?

4. Hold the magnet over the screw. What happens?

5. Hold the magnet over the barrette. What happens?

Write About It

Make a chart. Next to each object, put a check under *moves* or *does not move*.

Object	Moves	Does Not Move
button		
penny		
paper clip		
screw		
barrette		

Push and Pull for Fun

These people are having fun.

Which pictures show a push?
Who is pushing?

Which pictures show a pull?
What is pulling?

Which picture shows a father
pulling a swing?

Which picture shows a father
pushing a swing?

Think About It

Name a game
you play.

Tell how you
push or pull
when you play.

My Eighth Birthday

by Conchita Muñoz, age 8

When my birthday comes, my mom and I will invite my cousins to my birthday party. I will also invite my aunts and friends to my birthday party. My cousins and I will play tag and hide-and-seek.

Then we will eat. We will eat chicken and rice and a lot of other food.

After that we will break a piñata, and we will get a lot of candy. Then it will be time for my family to go home and my friends too. Then my mom and I will have to clean up.

That's what will happen at my birthday party.

Write About It

What kind of party would you like to have?

What would you eat? What games would you play?

Pulling and Pushing

by Frances Alexander

Pulling and pushing, my kingdom
was won.
Pushing and pulling, my kingdom
was gone.
When I tell you to push, be sure
that you pull.
When I tell you to pull, be sure
that you push.
Push! Pull!

Try It Out

Say the chant again. This time use your hands to show push or pull.

Tell what you learned.

1. Tell a friend about some things you play with that move.

2. Work in groups. Take turns moving things. Have your classmates describe your movements.

3. Draw a picture to show what the children did to break the piñata. Describe your picture.

CHAPTER 7

Plants We Eat

Tell what you know.

Do you like eating fruit?

Where do we get the fruit we eat?

Strawberries
$1.49/pint

3

2

4

Talk About It

How do strawberries get to your table?

What other fruits can you name?

117

What are the parts of a plant?

Name each plant.

What parts of each plant
do you see?

▲ broccoli

◀ coconut
palm

◀ corn

▲ cabbage

▲ rice

fruit ▲

leaves ▲

trunk ▶

The parts of plants
do different things.

Plants need water to live.
Roots take water from
the ground.

The trunk of a tree is a stem.
Stems carry water from the roots
to other parts of plants.

Plants need food too.
Leaves make food from sunlight.

? Think About It

Why do plants need roots?

What do the leaves of plants do?

roots

You can grow a plant.

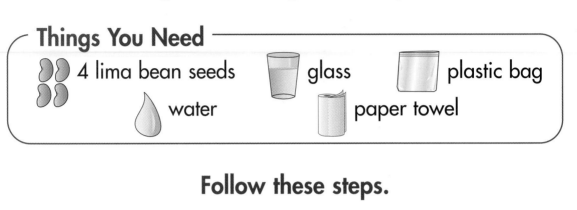

Things You Need

4 lima bean seeds

water

glass

paper towel

plastic bag

Follow these steps.

1. Put the 4 lima bean seeds into a glass with water.

2. Wait one day.

3. Put a wet paper towel inside a plastic bag.

4. Put the 4 lima bean seeds on top of the towel.

5. Watch the seeds for a few days.

6. Keep a record. What happens to your seeds? Write about your plants.

My Record

The parts of the plant that grew first were _____.

I saw roots _____.

I saw leaves _____.

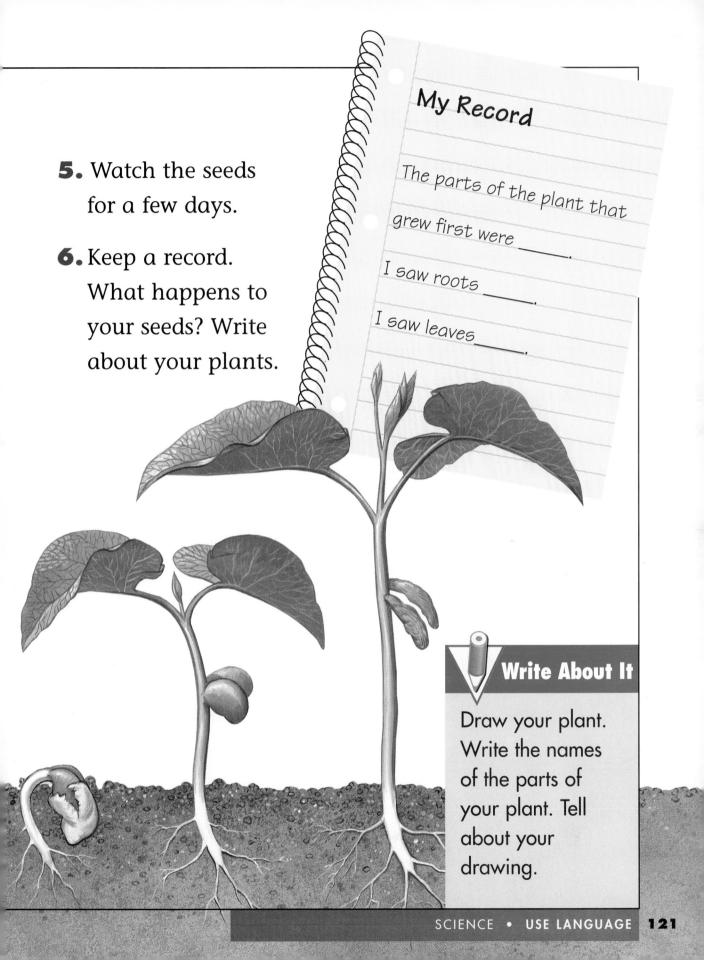

Write About It

Draw your plant. Write the names of the parts of your plant. Tell about your drawing.

What parts of plants do we eat?

People grow plants for food.
What plants did you eat yesterday?

Did you have celery, lettuce,
tomatoes, or carrots?
Each food is a different part
of a plant.

Celery is the stem of a plant.

Lettuce is the leaf of a plant.

A tomato is the fruit of a plant.
The seeds of a plant are in the fruit.

A carrot is the root of a plant.

stem ▶

fruit ▼

leaf ▶

root ▶

Name these foods.

Word Bank

apple

beans

broccoli

cabbage

corn

cucumber

orange

peach

radish

Write About It

Make a chart.
Write the name of a plant you eat.

Write it under the part of the plant you eat.

seed	root	stem	leaf	flower	fruit
beans					

Grains Around the World

Grains are important plants.
Most people in the world
eat grain.
Wheat, corn, rice, rye, oats, and
barley are grains.

Bread is made from grain.
Bread is made from wheat, rye,
corn, or barley.

Noodles are made
from grain.
Noodles are made from
wheat or rice.

RICE

1 lb.
net wt.

Tortillas are made from grain.
Tortillas are made from corn
or wheat.

Cereals are made from grain.
Oatmeal is made from oats.
Cornflakes are made from corn.

Popcorn is made from corn too!

Talk About It

What foods made from grains
do you eat?

What other foods are made from grains?

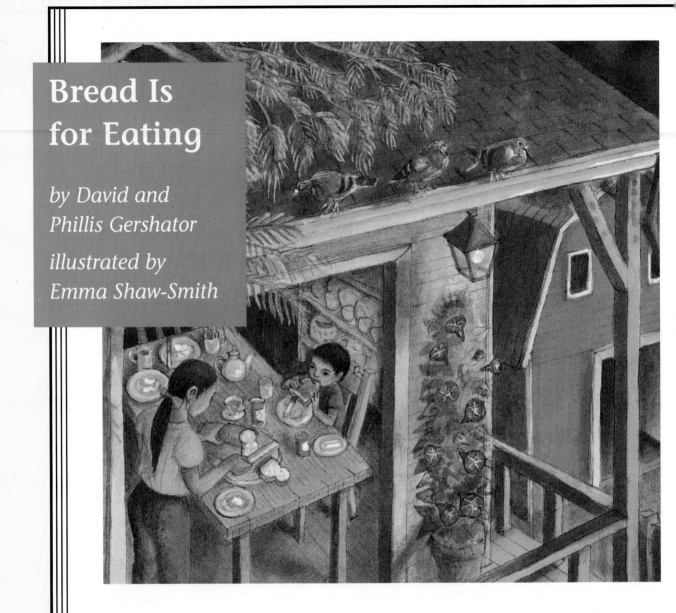

Bread Is for Eating

by David and Phillis Gershator

illustrated by Emma Shaw-Smith

"Bread is for eating," Mamita says when I leave bread on my plate. "Bread is for eating!" And she sings this song to me:

"El pan es para comer. El pan es para la vida. ¡No tires el pan! ¡Ay, ay! Vida mía."

"Think of the seed, asleep in the ground.
Think of the earth, a dark, cozy bed."

"Think of the sun, shining down on the earth.
Think of the rain, waking the seed from its
slumber."

"I'm thinking, Mamita. I'm thinking about the little sprouts coming up from the ground." And Mamita says, "This song is for the sprouting seed:

"*El pan es para comer. El pan es para la vida. ¡No tires el pan! ¡Ay, ay! Vida mía.*"

"Think of the farmer, who tills the soil, hoping
the rains will come on time.

Think of the harvester, who cuts the wheat
and catches the grain."

"Is it time for a song—a song for the grains
of wheat?"

*"El pan es para comer. El pan es para la vida.
¡No tires el pan! ¡Ay, ay! Vida mía."*

"Think of the worker, who loads the grain and takes it to town.

Think of the miller, who grinds grain into flour, so soft and fine. Think of the storekeeper, who sells us the flour."

"Yes, I'm thinking, Mamita. I'm thinking about the money we need to buy flour." And Mamita says, "This song is also for the families working all day to put bread on the table:

"*El pan es para comer. El pan es para la vida. ¡No tires el pan! ¡Ay, ay! Vida mía.*"

"Think of the cook, kneading flour with water and yeast. Think of the baker, baking bread before dawn."

"Think of the people around the world, dreaming of bread."

"I'm hungry for bread, Mamita," I say.

"Then toast it and butter it or spread it with jam.
Eat it cold, eat it hot. Eat a little, eat a lot.
¡El pan es bueno!"

"We thank the seed, earth, sun, and rain for the grain, the beautiful grain, and sing for the bread that gives us life again and again and again."

"Will you sing the song with me?"

"El pan es para comer.
El pan es para la vida.
¡No tires el pan!
¡Ay, ay! Vida mía."

OATS, PEAS, BEANS, AND BARLEY GROW

Oats, peas, beans, and barley grow,

Oats, peas, beans, and barley grow,

Can you or I or anyone know

How oats, peas, beans, and
barley grow?

Tell what you learned.

1. Make a chart. List each plant you ate last week. Write the part of the plant you ate.

Plants I Ate	Part I Ate

2. What does a plant need to live?

3. Draw one of the workers the story tells about. Put a title on your picture. Tell what that worker does.

CHAPTER
8

Where We Buy Food

Tell what you know.

What foods do you like to eat?
What can you buy at each place?

▼ bakery

Celia's Bakery

HOT DOGS

▲ ice cream truck

hot dog stand ▲

farmers' market ►

▼ supermarket

▼ grocery store

Sanchez Grocery

▼ butcher shop

SAM'S MEATS

SALE

EGGS
49¢

MILK
89¢ ½ gal

Talk About It

Where does your family buy food?

Where do people in other countries buy food?

141

Food From Farms

Where do stores get the food you buy?

Farmers grow **crops** on **farms**.

Sometimes customers drive to a farm in the country.

They enjoy seeing a farm.

They enjoy buying fresh fruits and vegetables.

What can they buy at this **farm stand?**

Word Bank

carrots

peas

plums

squash

tomatoes

Write About It

Write a letter to a friend. Tell about a farm stand.

From Farms to Customers

Most of the time customers buy food near their homes.

This is a **farmers' market** in the city.

Farmers bring food and plants to this market. Customers enjoy buying foods and plants that come directly from a farm.

What can they buy at this farmers' market?

USE LANGUAGE • SOCIAL STUDIES

This is a **supermarket.** All food comes to supermarkets on trucks. The trucks get some food from ships, trains, and planes.

Customers can buy food from all over the world. Bananas may come from Costa Rica, cocoa from Ghana, and coconuts from the Philippines.

Supermarkets let customers buy all their food in one place.

? Think About It

What other foods grow outside the United States?

Let's Eat

Where do you like to eat?

What foods do you like to eat there?

fast-food restaurant ▲

restaurant ▲

▼ cafeteria

Get 'Em Here

by Lee Bennett Hopkins

"Hot dogs with sauerkraut
Cold drinks here!
Hot dogs with sauerkraut
Get 'em here!
Hot dogs with sauerkraut
Cold drinks here!"

Shouts the man as he rolls the city's
            smallest store
                All tucked neatly
                    under a huge,
                        blue-and-orange-
                            striped umbrella.

Try It Out

Use the first 6 lines of the chant. Make up a new chant about your favorite foods and drinks. Share your chant with a partner.

What would you do if . . . ?

What would you do if you had two bananas and your friend didn't have any?

I'd eat one banana and give the other one to my friend.

Work in pairs. Answer the
questions.

1. What would you do if you had
four cookies and your friend
didn't have any?

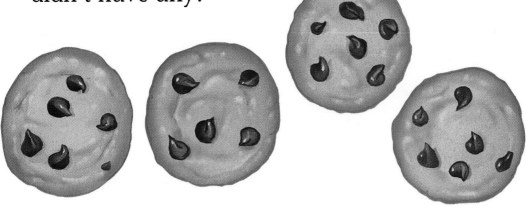

2. What would you do if you had
six strawberries and your friend
didn't have any?

 Think About It

What food would
you like to share
with your class?

How much of it
would you need
to bring?

Lee's Market

Sale This Week

pears **30¢** each

bananas **10¢** each

oranges **40¢** each

corn **20¢** each

apples **20¢** each

potatoes $1.25 a bag

beans 75¢ a bag

cabbage $1.00 a head

lemons 35¢ each

peas 89¢ a bag

strawberries (large) 5¢ each

peaches 50¢ each

Recipe: Fruit Salad

Serves 8

Ingredients

2 apples

2 bananas

2 pears

2 peaches

juice of 1 lemon

juice of 2 oranges

1/2 cup of sugar

6 large strawberries

Directions

Cut up all the fruit into small pieces. Put them into a bowl. Add the lemon juice, orange juice, and sugar. Mix. Put the bowl into the refrigerator for one hour.

Try It Out

You want to make the fruit salad recipe. You are going to Lee's Market.

What kinds of fruits do you need to buy? How many do you need to buy of each?

How much money do you need to buy all the fruit?

GROWING SONG

Navajo Indian

My great corn plants,
Among them I walk.
I speak to them;
They hold out their hands to me.

My great squash vines,
Among them I walk.
I speak to them;
They hold out their hands to me.

? Think About It

Why do some people talk to plants?

What could you say to a plant in a garden?

Tell what you learned.

1. Where do you and your family buy food? Make a chart.

Where We Buy Food	What We Buy

2. Draw a picture about a time when you went with your family to buy food. Write about your picture.

3. Make an ad for a grocery store. Draw pictures and write names of foods. Then put prices in your ad.

CHAPTER 9

Day and Night

Tell what you know.

What do you see in the sky during the day?

What do you see in the sky at night?

Word Bank

clouds

moon

stars

sun

Star Light, Star Bright

Star light, star bright,
First star I see tonight,
I wish I may,
I wish I might,
Have the wish
I wish tonight.

? Think About It

Which goes faster for you—day or night?

When did you wish for time to go faster?

How do day and night happen?

The sun lights the **earth.**
But the earth is always turning.

The part of the earth that faces the
sun has **day.**

The part of the earth that faces
away from the sun has **night.**

Earth

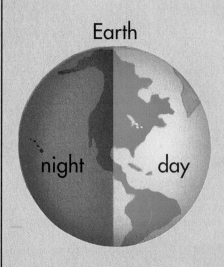

night

day

sun

It takes 24 **hours** for the earth to make one turn. So, there are 24 hours in one day.

It is **light** outside for part of each day. It is **dark** outside for part of each day.

Talk About It

What do you do when it is light outside?

What do you do when it is dark outside?

What is the sun?

The sun is a star.
It is the star closest to the earth.

The sun is made of
very hot gases.
It is shaped like a ball.

The sun gives the
earth light.
The sun gives the
earth **heat.**

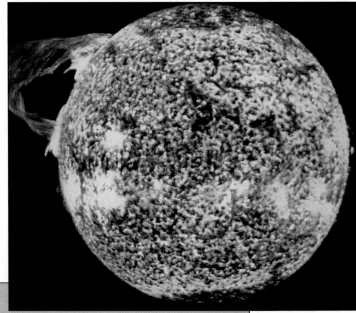

What can the sun do?

Things You Need

 2 plates timer 2 ice cubes

Follow these steps.

1. Put an ice cube on each plate.

2. Put one plate in a place that gets sunlight.

3. Put the other plate in a place that doesn't get sunlight.

4. Use the timer. How long does each ice cube take to melt?

My Record

The ice cube that was in the sunlight _____.

The ice cube that was not in the sunlight _____.

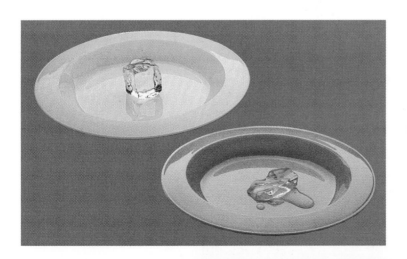

Think About It

Why would you keep a cold drink out of the sunlight?

What is the moon like?

The moon has no water.
The moon has no air.
The moon has only rocks and soil.

Can people, plants, or animals
live on the moon?

The moon circles the earth.
It takes about one **month** for the
moon to move around the earth.

There are 12 months in a **year.**

Old Man Moon

by *Aileen Fisher*

The moon is very,
very old.
The reason why is clear—
he gets a birthday
once a month,
instead of once a year.

Try It Out

If you were one year old, how many
months old would you be?

How many months old are you now?

How did people measure time long ago?

Long, long ago in Egypt, people watched the sun, the moon, and the stars. They wrote about what they saw.

They found that there are about 365 days in a year. They found that there are about 30 days in a month.

Long, long ago
in Central America,
people watched the
sun and the moon.
They wrote about what they saw.

They found that there are about
365 days in a year.

Today, in the United States, we use
a calendar like these old ones.
It has about 365 days in a year.
It has about 30 days in a month.

Think About It

Why is it
important to have
a calendar?

What other ways
do you tell time?

Nine O'Clock Lullaby

written by
Marilyn Singer
illustrated by
Frané Lessac

9 P.M. in Brooklyn, New York

The vroom and shush of traffic outside
the bedroom window while Mama turns
the pages of a sleepytime tale.
9 P.M. in Brooklyn, New York, is . . .

10 P.M. in Puerto Rico

Sweet rice, fruit ice, coconut candy. Papa
playing congas, Tío his guitar. Swaying
lanterns in the branches, dancing people
on the grass. Bedtime is forgotten on a
special party night.

10 P.M. in Puerto Rico is . . .

Midnight on the mid-Atlantic

Nothing blacker than the water, nothing
wider than the sky. Pitch and toss, pitch
and toss. The Big Dipper might just ladle
a drink out of the sea.

Midnight on the mid-Atlantic is . . .

2 A.M. in England

Bread in the pantry at nighttime
tastes better than cream cakes at tea.
2 A.M. in England is . . .

3 A.M. in Zaire

Dreaming by the Congo.

3 A.M. in Switzerland

Dreaming in the Alps.
3 A.M. in Zaire and Switzerland is . . .

5 A.M. in Moscow

A crash and a clatter and the samovar on the floor.
The cat has done it again! Papa wakes up with a
laugh. Mama wakes up with a shout. Babushka
doesn't wake at all, but just stays snoring in her bed.
5 A.M. in Moscow, Russia, is . . .

7:30 A.M. in India

All over the village well ropes
squeak, buckets splash, bracelets
jingle, long braids swish. All over
the village morning music.
7:30 A.M. in India is . . .

10 A.M. in Guangzhou, China

On the way to Goat City auntie pedals quickly, flying like a dragon. On the way to Goat City elder sister pedals slowly, flapping like a goose. 10 A.M. in Guangzhou, China, is . . .

11 A.M. in Japan

In the pond
   grandfather floats a tulip
      so the fish can greet the spring.
11 A.M. in Japan is . . .

Noon in Sydney, Australia

At the barbie, five cousins, four
uncles, three aunts, two sheepdogs,
six lizards, and one sly kookaburra
stealing sausage right off the plates.
Noon in Sydney, Australia, is . . .

3 P.M. in Samoa

The rain has stopped. The sea is calm.
"Let's weave," say the mothers. "Let's fish,"
say the fathers. "Let's chase the dogs," say
the brothers, "before it rains again."
3 P.M. in Samoa is . . .

5 P.M. in Nome, Alaska

Toss the blanket high. Toss the
blanket higher. Ask her, can
she see the caribou? Ask her,
can she touch the sky?
5 P.M. in Nome, Alaska, is . . .

6 P.M. in Los Angeles

The sun eases down like a big golden dinner
plate at the end of the day on the beach.
6 P.M. in Los Angeles is . . .

8 P.M. in Mexico

Saying good night to the burros

8 P.M. in Wisconsin

Saying good night to the calves
8 P.M. in Mexico and Wisconsin is . . .

9 P.M. in Brooklyn, New York

The vroom and shush of traffic outside the bedroom
window while Mama turns the pages of a sleepytime tale.

Out in the Dark and Daylight

by Aileen Fisher

Out in the dark and daylight,
under a cloud or tree,

Out in the park and play light,
out where the wind blows free,

Out in the March or May light
with shadows and stars to see,

Out in the dark and daylight . . .
that's where I like to be.

Write About It

How do you feel
when it's dark?

Tell what you learned.

1. Work with a group. List things the sun can do.

2. Work with a partner. Write a question about the moon. Ask the class your question.

3. Choose an hour from the story. Draw a picture. Show something you do at that time. Put a title on your picture. Tell a classmate about your picture.

Long Ago and Today

Tell what you know.

Which clocks were used long ago?

Which clocks are used today?

Which clocks do you use?

hourglass ▶

sundial
▼

▲ clock

◄ watches

Word Bank

o'clock

one

two

three

four

five

six

seven

eight

nine

ten

eleven

twelve

watch ▲

◄ pendulum
clock

Talk About It

What time is it now?

What time will it be when you leave school today?

What was it like in this country long ago?

The first people in North America were Indians.

About 500 years ago, people from other countries began to come to North America.

People came from Spain to look for gold.

Later, more Spanish people came to settle the land. The settlers lived in settlements.

Look at the map.

Can you name some early Spanish settlements?

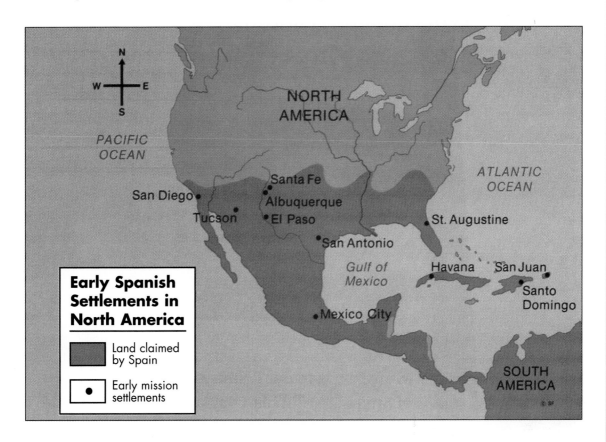

The Spanish settlers and the Indians learned new things from each other.

The Indians taught the Spanish about new plants.

Many Indians learned to speak Spanish.

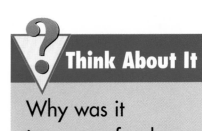

Think About It

Why was it important for the Indians and the Spanish people to learn each other's language?

Who were the next settlers?

About 400 years ago, the Pilgrims came to North America from England. They came on ships. The first ship was called the *Mayflower*.

Their first winter was hard. It was cold. The Pilgrims didn't have enough to eat. Many Pilgrims died.

In the spring, the Indians helped the Pilgrims plant crops.

During the summer, the crops grew. The Pilgrims had a lot of food that year.

In the fall, the Pilgrims asked the Indians to share a meal with them. They thanked God for their friends and food. This was the first Thanksgiving.

Think About It

The Indians helped the Pilgrims. Who helps newcomers today?

What holidays do people celebrate in this country?

We celebrate old **holidays.**

We celebrate Thanksgiving Day on the fourth Thursday in November.

How do people celebrate Thanksgiving today? What do you think people are thankful for today?

We celebrate new holidays.

We celebrate Martin Luther King Day on the third Monday in January.

Dr. Martin Luther King, Jr., helped people. African Americans were not treated fairly. He dreamed that all people would be treated fairly. He told people about his dream. His dream helped change things.

Talk About It

What holidays do you like to celebrate? Tell about them.

A Look at the Calendar

How many holidays are marked in May? On which day is Cinco de Mayo celebrated? On which day is Memorial Day celebrated?

How many holidays are marked in June? On which day is Flag Day celebrated?

CONNECT LANGUAGE • SOCIAL STUDIES/MATH

How many holidays are marked in July? On which day is Independence Day celebrated?

Which month doesn't have any holidays marked?

Word Bank

January

February

March

April

May

June

July

August

September

October

November

December

Talk About It

In which month do you celebrate your birthday? Are there any holidays celebrated in the month of your birthday?

My Favorite Holiday

by Thao Ngo, age 8

In Vietnam, Têt is the start of a new year.

On Têt my mom gives me $2.00 in Vietnamese money.

My mom buys watermelon and cuts it up. My baby sister, my brothers, my mom, my dad, and I eat it. I like to eat watermelon. We also eat a special big cake on Têt.

Then my mom and dad go buy firecrackers. My dog is scared of the firecrackers. He won't go outside when we light them. The best part of Têt is the firecrackers. I like them very much.

Talk About It

Tell about a holiday you celebrate with your family. What special foods do you like to eat?

Bells Are Ringing
(an Eastern European round)

When on New Year's,
   in the morning,
Bells are ringing, people bringing,
Clear bells, sweet bells,
Bim, Bom, Bim, Bom!

In the evening, gently tolling,
Sweetly knelling, gladly telling,
Work is ended.
Bim, Bom, Bim, Bom!

Write About It

Draw a picture of how you celebrate the new year. Write about your picture.

Tell what you learned.

1. Work with a partner. Make a map that shows early Spanish settlements.

2. Act out a scene from early America. Show one way the Indians helped the Pilgrims after their first hard winter.

3. Draw a picture to show how you celebrate one holiday. Write about your picture. Share your picture with a classmate.

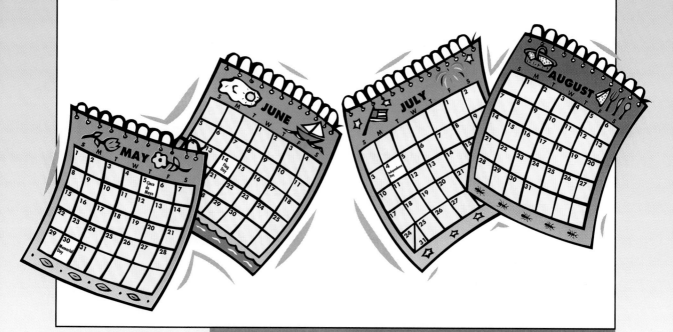

CHAPTER 11

Where We Find Water

Tell what you know.

How do people use water?

How do you use water?

Word Bank

drinking

fishing

swimming

washing

watering

 Think About It

What would you do without water?

What would the earth be like without water? Draw a picture.

Bodies of Water

Where can you find water?

You can find water in a **pond.**
A pond is a small body of water.
What are these people doing at
this pond?

You can find water
in a **lake.**
A lake is a body of
water that is larger
than a pond.
What are these people
doing in this lake?

You can find water in a **river.**
A river is a body of moving water.
What are these people doing on
this river?

You can find water
in an **ocean.** An
ocean is a very large
body of water. The
water in an ocean is
salty. What are
these people doing
on this ocean?

Where are bodies of water in the United States?

Word Bank

east

north

south

west

The United States

CANADA

WASHINGTON

Columbia R.

OREGON

IDAHO

Snake R.

MONTANA

Missouri R.

NORTH DAKOTA

MINNESOT

SOUTH DAKOTA

WYOMING

NORTH PLATTE R.

NEBRASKA

IOW

Sacramento R.

Great Salt Lake

NEVADA

UTAH

Green R.

South Platte R.

Platte R.

Missouri R.

San Joaquin R.

CALIFORNIA

COLORADO

Colorado R.

KANSAS

Arkansas R.

PACIFIC OCEAN

ARIZONA

NEW MEXICO

OKLAHOMA

Rio Grande

TEXAS

Brazos R.

ARCTIC OCEAN

RUSSIA

HAWAII

Yukon R.

ALASKA

CANADA

MEXICO

BERING SEA

PACIFIC OCEAN

GULF OF ALASKA

Study the map with a partner.

1. Think about where you live. Write the direction you would go to see the Atlantic Ocean.

2. List 2 states that are on the Pacific Ocean.

3. List 3 states along the Mississippi River.

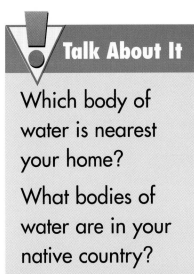

Talk About It

Which body of water is nearest your home?

What bodies of water are in your native country?

Do people have enough water?

Some people live where there is a lot of water.

Some people live where there is little water.

Word Bank

dry

flood

wet

 **Write About It**

Tell about a time when you saw too much rain or too little rain.

What happens when there is too much rain?

What happens if there is not enough rain?

In some places it does not rain for days, weeks, or months.

If this happens, lakes and rivers may dry up. Plants may not get the water they need to grow. Animals may not have plants to eat. People may not have the water they need.

Saving Water

Things You Need

faucet

cup

Follow these steps.

1. Turn on a faucet until it drips.

2. Let the water drip into a cup.

3. Wait 5 minutes. How much water is in the cup?

My Record

After 5 minutes I saw ____.

The dripping faucet wasted ____.

Think About It

How can people save water?

Brave Dog

*Story by
Cynthia Rylant*

*Pictures by
Suçie Stevenson*

For lunch,
Henry and Mudge
and Henry's father
walked to a hot dog stand.

Henry had a hot dog
with ketchup.
Henry's father had a hot dog
with ketchup
and mustard
and onions
and slaw
and chili
and cheese.

"Yuck," said Henry.

Mudge had three hot dogs.

Plain.

In one gulp.

After lunch,
Henry and his father
began to build
a sand castle.

Henry made the moats.

Henry's father made the towers.

Mudge made a nice bed

and went to sleep.

When the castle was finished,

Henry's father

stuck his red rubber lobster

on the tallest tower.

Then he and Henry

clapped their hands.

Suddenly
a giant wave
washed far on the sand
and it covered everything.
It covered the moats.
It covered the towers.

It covered Mudge, who woke up.

"Oops," said Henry.

"Save that lobster!"
cried Henry's father.
The water was pulling it
out to sea.

Mudge ran and jumped
into the waves.
He caught the lobster
before it was lost forever.

"Good dog!" said Henry's father.

"Brave dog!" said Henry.

They all had cherry sno-cones

to celebrate.

Sitting in the Sand

by Karla Kuskin

Sitting in the sand and the sea
    comes up
So you put your hands together
And you use them like a cup
And you dip them in the water
With a scooping kind of motion
And before the sea goes out again
You have a sip of ocean.

Think About It

Would you want
to sip the ocean?
Why not?

Tell what you learned.

1. Work with a group. Make two lists. Then share your lists with other groups.

Ways We Use Water
_____
_____
_____

Ways We Save Water
_____
_____
_____

2. Work with a friend. Use a map of the United States. Choose a place you and your friend would like to visit that is near the Atlantic or Pacific Ocean. Trace the path you would follow. Which direction would you go?

3. Tell something that Henry and Mudge did. What would you like to do at the beach?

Water and the Weather

Tell what you know.

How does rain make people feel?

How does rain make you feel?

Rain on the green grass,
And rain on the tree,
Rain on the housetop,
But not on me.

Word Bank

clouds

drizzle

puddle

rainbow

storm

Talk About It

Tell about a time
when you enjoyed
rain.

217

Clouds in the Sky

Sometimes there are white clouds in the sky.

Sometimes there are dark clouds in the sky.

When there are dark clouds in the sky, it may rain.

Clouds are made of drops of water.
It rains when drops of water from
the clouds fall to the ground.

Word Bank

lightning

thunder

cloudy

gray

windy

Think About It

How can you tell
when it's going
to rain?

Water in the Air

Fill a glass with ice water.
Wait 5 minutes.
What do you see?

The drops of water on the glass
came from water in the air.
You cannot see this water in the air.
It is called **water vapor.**

The glass cooled the water vapor
around it.
The cooled water vapor changed
to drops of water.

Have you seen a puddle after
it rains?
How does the puddle look?
How does the puddle look after the
sun has been out for a while?
The water in the puddle dries up.
The water goes into the air.

Think About It

When your hair
is wet, it dries
after a while.
Where does the
water go?

The Water Cycle

Water falls from clouds to the earth.

Then it rises from the earth to form new clouds.

This is called the **water cycle.**

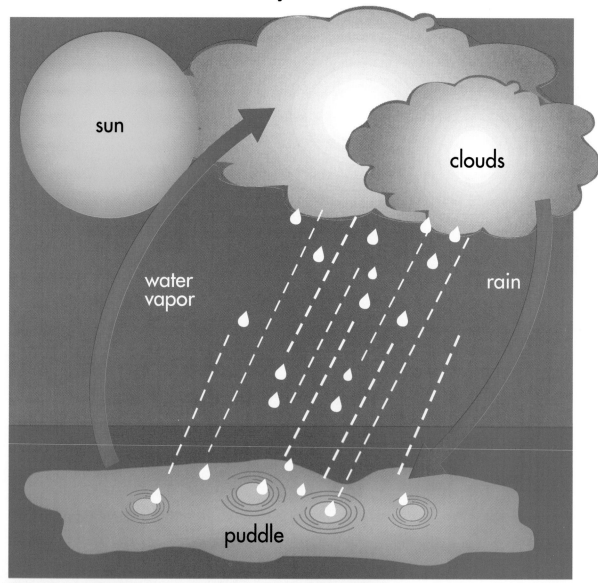

You can make a cloud.

Things You Need

jar

very warm water

ice cubes

metal lid

Follow these steps.

1. Rinse the jar in warm water.

2. Put a little warm water in the jar.

3. Place the lid upside down on top of the jar.

4. Put the ice cubes on the lid.

5. See what happens in the jar.

My Record

When I put the ice cubes on the lid, I saw _____.

How much rain?

In Kim's city by the ocean, it rained 4 inches one week, 4 inches the second week, and 1 inch during the third week. How much rain fell in three weeks?

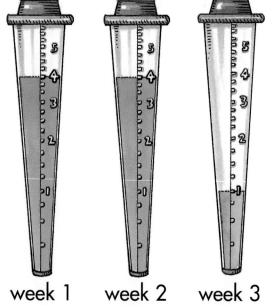

week 1   week 2   week 3

In Maria's desert city, it rained 1 inch in the fall, 1 inch in the winter, and 4 inches in the spring. It did not rain in the summer. How much rain fell this year?

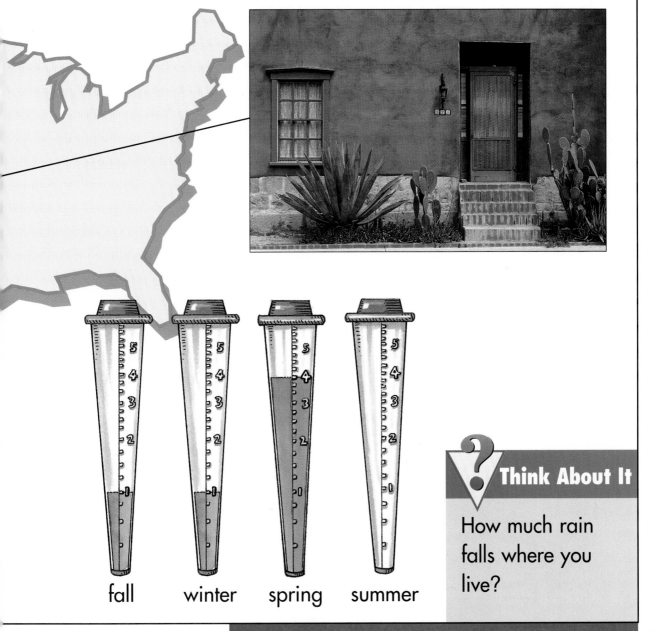

fall   winter   spring   summer

? Think About It

How much rain falls where you live?

©1995 United Feature Syndicate, Inc.

Think About It

Why is this cartoon funny?

Water Cartoons

Think about times when you use water.

Did something funny happen as you washed dishes?

Did something funny happen as you took a bath?

Did something funny happen when you went swimming?

Did something funny happen as you walked in the rain?

Work with a partner. Make a list of times when you use water. Then together make up a cartoon about water.

Raindrops

by Clara Belle Baker

Patter pat, patter pat,
What a gentle sound is that!
Patter pat, patter pat,
Hear the raindrops tap!

Now the grass and flow'rs will be
Fresh and bright for you to see!
Patter, pat, patter pat,
Hear the raindrops tap!

Try It Out

Sing the song. Use hand and arm motions to act out what the rain does.

Tell what you learned.

1. Make a chart. Tell what the weather will probably be.

Clouds	Weather
white clouds	
dark clouds	

2. Work with a group. Make a mural of the water cycle. Tell about it.

3. Work with some friends. Draw a picture together to show what is happening in "Raindrops." Then sing the song or take turns telling about it.

Writer's Workshop

Follow these steps to be a good writer.

❶ Prewriting

Choose a topic.
Write your ideas.

Animals

fish
bird
bear
cat
woodchuck
turtle
spider

Organize your ideas.

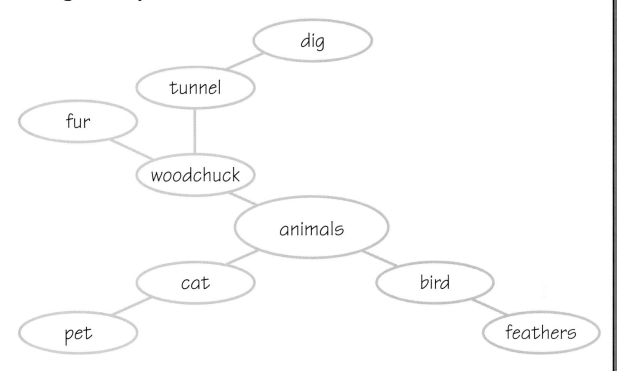

Choose one idea.

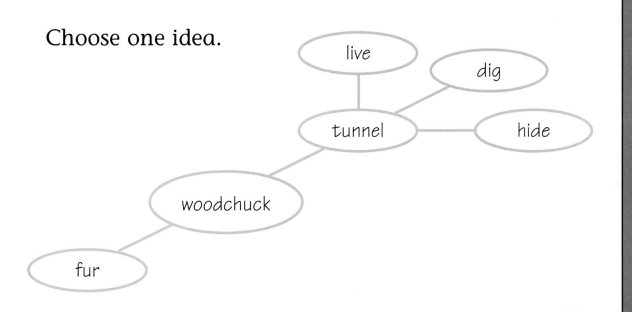

② Writing

Write about your idea.

Woodchucks dig tunnel.
They use their feet.
Live in tunnels.
woodchucks have fur.
Woodchucks protect itself in tunnel

❸ Revising

Read your story.

Can you make it better?

Can a friend help you make it better?

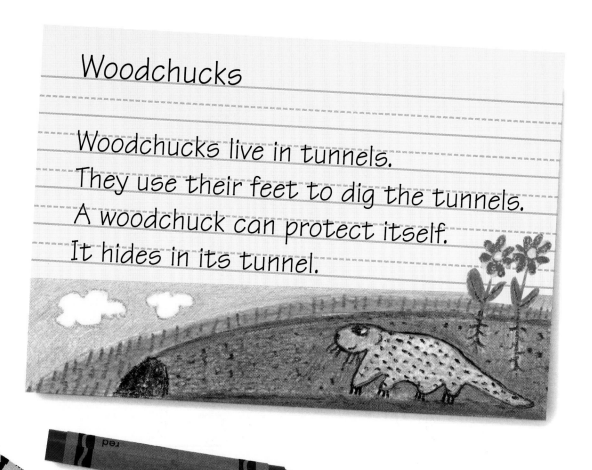

Woodchucks

Woodchucks live in tunnels.
They use their feet to dig the tunnels.
A woodchuck can protect itself.
It hides in its tunnel.

④ Presenting

Read your story aloud.

Put your story in a book.

What a Good Writer Can Do

- I can plan before I write.

- I can write about things I know. I can write about animals, my family, and myself.

- I can write stories with a beginning, a middle, and an end.

- I can ask others to read my work.

- I can write in complete sentences.

- I can put periods at the ends of sentences.

- I can make my handwriting easy to read.